Dear Parents,

Welcome to the Scholastic Reader series. We have taken over 80 years of experience with teachers, parents, and children and put it into a program that is designed to match your child's interests and skills.

Level 1—Short sentences and stories made up of words kids can sound out using their phonics skills and words that are important to remember.

Level 2—Longer sentences and stories with words kids need to know and new "big" words that they will want to know.

Level 3—From sentences to paragraphs to longer stories, these books have large "chunks" of texts and are made up of a rich vocabulary.

Level 4—First chapter books with more words and fewer pictures.

It is important that children learn to read well enough to succeed in school and beyond. Here are ideas for reading this book with your child:

- Look at the book together. Encourage your child to read the title and make a prediction about the story.
- Read the book together. Encourage your child to sound out words when appropriate. When your child struggles, you can help by providing the word.
- Encourage your child to retell the story. This is a great way to check for comprehension.
- Have your child take the fluency test on the last page to check progress.

Scholastic Readers are designed to support your child's efforts to learn how to read at every age and every stage. Enjoy helping your child learn to read and love to read.

> —**Francie Alexander**
> Chief Education Officer
> Scholastic Education

For Ian Michael Grant McPherson Ortiz — Welcome!
— J.M.

For Max Mindich
— W.W.

Text copyright © 2005 by Jean Marzollo.
"Toy Planet" from *I Spy Fantasy* © 1994 by Walter Wick; "A Secret Cupboard,"
"Good Morning," and "House on the Hill" from *I Spy Spooky Night* © 1996
by Walter Wick; "Arts & Crafts," "Toys in the Attic," and "Silhouettes" from *I Spy*
© 1992 by Walter Wick; "Levers, Ramps, and Pulleys" and "Patterns and Paint"
from *I Spy School Days* © 1995 by Walter Wick.
All rights reserved. Published by Scholastic Inc.
SCHOLASTIC, CARTWHEEL BOOKS, and associated logos are trademarks
and/or registered trademarks of Scholastic Inc.

Library of Congress Cataloging-in-Publication Data is available.

ISBN 0-439-73863-6

10 9 8 7 6 5 4 3 2 1   05 06 07 08 9/0
Printed in the U.S.A. 23
First printing, September 2005

I SPY

A PUMPKIN

Riddles by Jean Marzollo
Photographs by Walter Wick

Scholastic Reader — Level 1

SCHOLASTIC INC.

Cartwheel ·B·O·O·K·S· ®

New York Toronto London Auckland Sydney
Mexico City New Delhi Hong Kong Buenos Aires

I spy

 a pumpkin,

a bushy hare,

 a skull,

 a wagon,

and IF YOU DARE!

ENTER
IF YOU DARE!

I spy

a cardinal,

 a lion's mane,

french fries,

 a 5,

and a yellow
airplane.

I spy

the ocean,

a zebra,

a fan,

two jars of paint,

and a pipe-cleaner man.

I spy

a battery,

 a faded blue N,

two thimbles,

 a guitar,

a spring,

 and a hen.

I spy

a horse,

 a red-and-white ball,

a musical note,

and a train that's small.

I spy

an arrowhead,

 a ring,

a key,

 a piece to a puzzle,

a trophy,

 and a G.

I spy

a soccer ball,

 a dog,

a bee,

 a green-and-yellow dress,

and a pot of tea.

I spy

a ribbon,

a set of four,

a horse's wheels,

and a
GAME OF STORE.

I spy

 a sword,

a phone,

 a block T,

a trophy,

 a magnet,

a duck,

 and a wooden tree.

I spy

 a yellow car,

a playing-card tower,

 a lamb,

a phone,

 and a can of flour.

I spy two matching words.

yellow airplane

green-and-yellow dress

 set of four

I spy two words that start with the letter T.

two jars of paint

 can of flour

playing-card tower

I spy two matching words.

 soccer ball

pipe-cleaner man

 red-and-white ball

I spy two words that start with the letters TR.

lion's mane

wooden tree

 trophy

I spy two words that end with the letter Y.

battery

  thimbles

bushy hare

I spy two words that end
with the letters LL.

soccer ball

 french fries

train that's small

I spy two words that rhyme.

key

 musical note

pot of tea

I spy two words that rhyme.

 a hen

arrowhead

 blue N

Collect all the I Spy Readers!

And the original I Spy books, too!

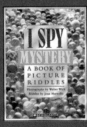 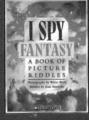 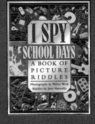   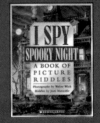 

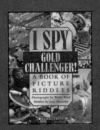